60
AND
PROUD
OF IT

summersdale

60 AND PROUD OF IT

Copyright © Summersdale Publishers Ltd, 2014

With text contributed by Vicky Edwards

Summersdale Publishers Ltd
46 West Street
Chichester
West Sussex
PO19 1RP
UK

www.summersdale.com

Printed and bound in the Czech Republic

ISBN: 978-1-84953-564-9

Substantial discounts on bulk quantities of Summersdale books are available to corporations, professional associations and other organisations. For details contact Nicky Douglas by telephone: +44 (0) 1243 756902, fax: +44 (0) 1243 786300 or email: nicky@summersdale.com.

TO...

FROM.......................................

CONTENTS

ANOTHER
YEAR
OLDER

I'M 60 YEARS OF AGE.
THAT'S 16 CELSIUS!

George Carlin

OUR BIRTHDAYS ARE FEATHERS IN THE BROAD WING OF TIME.

Jean Paul

THE BEST BIRTHDAYS OF ALL ARE THOSE THAT HAVEN'T ARRIVED YET.

Robert Orben

YOU ARE NEVER TOO OLD TO SET ANOTHER GOAL OR TO DREAM A NEW DREAM.

C. S. Lewis

THERE WAS A STAR DANCED, AND UNDER THAT WAS I BORN.

William Shakespeare

ON THE LAST DAY OF
MY FIFTY-NINTH YEAR
I WAS TREMBLING WITH
ANTICIPATION. I'VE
HEARD SO MUCH ABOUT
THE SWINGING SIXTIES –
I COULDN'T WAIT TO
GET STUCK IN!

Anonymous

SOME PEOPLE REACH
THE AGE OF 60
BEFORE OTHERS.

Lord Hood

I WAS ALWAYS TAUGHT TO
RESPECT MY ELDERS AND
I'VE NOW REACHED THE
AGE WHEN I DON'T HAVE
ANYBODY TO RESPECT.

George Burns

THE OLDER THE FIDDLE, THE SWEETER THE TUNE.

English proverb

YOU'RE NOT 60. YOU'RE
18 WITH 42 YEARS OF
EXPERIENCE.

Anonymous

FROM OUR BIRTHDAY,
UNTIL WE DIE,
IS BUT THE WINKING
OF AN EYE.

W. B. Yeats

YOU CAN'T TURN BACK
THE CLOCK, BUT YOU CAN
WIND IT UP AGAIN.

Bonnie Prudden

EVERY YEAR ON YOUR
BIRTHDAY, YOU GET A
CHANCE TO START NEW.

Sammy Hagar

WHATEVER WITH THE PAST HAS GONE, THE BEST IS ALWAYS YET TO COME.

Lucy Larcom

I HAVE EVERYTHING I HAD 20 YEARS AGO, ONLY IT'S ALL A LITTLE BIT LOWER.

Gypsy Rose Lee

PLEAS'D TO LOOK
FORWARD, PLEAS'D TO
LOOK BEHIND,
AND COUNT EACH
BIRTHDAY WITH A
GRATEFUL MIND.

Alexander Pope

THE IMPORTANT THING
IS NOT HOW MANY YEARS
IN YOUR LIFE BUT
HOW MUCH LIFE
IN YOUR YEARS.

Edward Stieglitz

JUST
WHAT
I ALWAYS
WANTED

A HUG IS THE PERFECT
GIFT; ONE SIZE FITS ALL,
AND NOBODY MINDS IF
YOU EXCHANGE IT.

Anonymous

YOU KNOW YOU ARE
GETTING OLD WHEN THE
CANDLES COST MORE
THAN THE CAKE.

Bob Hope

YESTERDAY IS HISTORY, TOMORROW IS A MYSTERY, BUT TODAY IS A GIFT. THAT IS WHY IT IS CALLED THE PRESENT.

Anonymous

IF INSTEAD OF A GEM,
OR EVEN A FLOWER, WE
SHOULD CAST THE GIFT
OF A LOVING THOUGHT
INTO THE HEART OF A
FRIEND, THAT WOULD
BE GIVING AS THE
ANGELS GIVE.

George MacDonald

YOUTH IS THE GIFT OF NATURE, BUT AGE IS A WORK OF ART.

Garson Kanin

THE ABILITY TO
LAUGH, ESPECIALLY AT
OURSELVES, KEEPS THE
HEART LIGHT AND THE
MIND YOUNG.

Anonymous

THERE ARE 364 DAYS
WHEN YOU MIGHT
GET UN-BIRTHDAY
PRESENTS... AND ONLY
ONE FOR BIRTHDAY
PRESENTS, YOU KNOW.

Lewis Carroll

A GIFT, WITH A KIND
COUNTENANCE, IS A
DOUBLE PRESENT.

Proverb

A TRUE FRIEND REMEMBERS YOUR BIRTHDAY BUT NOT YOUR AGE.

Anonymous

BIRTHDAYS ARE GOOD
FOR YOU. STATISTICS
SHOW THAT THE PEOPLE
WHO HAVE THE MOST
LIVE THE LONGEST.

Larry Lorenzoni

SURPRISE IS THE GREATEST GIFT WHICH LIFE CAN GRANT US.

Boris Pasternak

NOBODY CAN BE
UNCHEERED WITH
A BALLOON.

A. A. Milne

A BIRTHDAY IS JUST THE
FIRST DAY OF ANOTHER
365-DAY JOURNEY
AROUND THE SUN.
ENJOY THE TRIP.

Anonymous

GRIN AND BEAR IT

SIXTY IS THE NEW FORTY!

Bill Maher

'AGE' IS THE
ACCEPTANCE OF A
TERM OF YEARS. BUT
MATURITY IS THE GLORY
OF YEARS.

Martha Graham

GETTING OLD IS A BIT
LIKE GETTING DRUNK;
EVERYONE ELSE LOOKS
BRILLIANT.

Billy Connolly

I STILL HAVE A FULL
DECK; I JUST SHUFFLE
SLOWER NOW.

Anonymous

AGE IS A MATTER OF FEELING, NOT OF YEARS.

George William Curtis

ONE STARTS TO GET
YOUNG AT THE AGE OF
60 AND THEN IT IS
TOO LATE.

Pablo Picasso

OLD AGE IS AN
EXCELLENT TIME FOR
OUTRAGE. MY GOAL IS
TO SAY OR DO AT LEAST
ONE OUTRAGEOUS THING
EVERY WEEK.

Maggie Kuhn

AGE IS AN ISSUE OF
MIND OVER MATTER.
IF YOU DON'T MIND, IT
DOESN'T MATTER.

Mark Twain

STOP WORRYING ABOUT
THE POTHOLES IN THE
ROAD AND CELEBRATE
THE JOURNEY!

Anonymous

MY IDEA OF HELL IS TO BE YOUNG AGAIN.

Marge Piercy

I SO ENJOY WAKING UP AND NOT HAVING TO GO TO WORK. SO I DO IT THREE OR FOUR TIMES A DAY.

Gene Perret

ONE OF THE BEST PARTS
OF GROWING OLDER?
YOU CAN FLIRT ALL
YOU LIKE SINCE YOU'VE
BECOME HARMLESS.

Liz Smith

THERE IS ALWAYS A LOT
TO BE THANKFUL FOR IF
YOU TAKE THE TIME TO
LOOK. FOR EXAMPLE, I'M
SITTING HERE THINKING
HOW NICE IT IS THAT
WRINKLES DON'T HURT.

Anonymous

IT'S SAD TO GROW OLD, BUT NICE TO RIPEN.

Brigitte Bardot

NO MATTER WHAT
HAPPENS, I'M LOUD,
NOISY, EARTHY AND
READY FOR MUCH
MORE LIVING.

Elizabeth Taylor

I'M NOT INTERESTED IN
AGE. PEOPLE WHO TELL
ME THEIR AGE ARE
SILLY. YOU'RE AS OLD
AS YOU FEEL.

Elizabeth Arden

DO A LITTLE DANCE, MAKE A LITTLE LOVE

GROW OLD ALONG
WITH ME!
THE BEST IS
YET TO BE.

Robert Browning

OLD AGE IS ALWAYS 15
YEARS OLDER THAN I AM.

Bernard Baruch

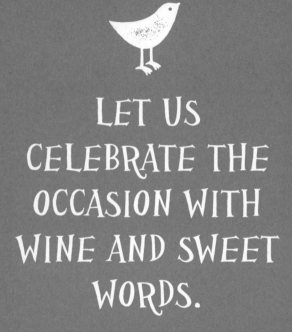

LET US CELEBRATE THE OCCASION WITH WINE AND SWEET WORDS.

Plautus

THE AGEING PROCESS
HAS YOU FIRMLY IN ITS
GRASP IF YOU NEVER
GET THE URGE TO
THROW A SNOWBALL.

Doug Larson

I CELEBRATE MYSELF, AND SING MYSELF.

Walt Whitman

THE OTHER DAY A MAN
ASKED ME WHAT I
THOUGHT WAS THE BEST
TIME OF LIFE. 'WHY,' I
ANSWERED WITHOUT A
THOUGHT, 'NOW.'

David Grayson

IT'S IMPORTANT TO HAVE A TWINKLE IN YOUR WRINKLE.

Anonymous

IT'S TIME TO START LIVING THE LIFE YOU'VE IMAGINED.

Henry James

AS THIS AUSPICIOUS DAY
BEGAN THE RACE OF
EV'RY VIRTUE JOIN'D
WITH EV'RY GRACE;
MAY YOU, WHO OWN
THEM, WELCOME
ITS RETURN, TILL
EXCELLENCE, LIKE
YOURS, AGAIN IS BORN.

Lord Francis Jeffrey

I ALWAYS MAKE A POINT
OF STARTING THE
DAY AT 6 A.M. WITH
CHAMPAGNE. IT GOES
STRAIGHT TO THE HEART
AND CHEERS ONE UP.
WHITE WINE WON'T DO.
YOU NEED THE BUBBLES.

John Mortimer

LIFE IS TOO SHORT, SO
KISS SLOWLY, LAUGH
INSANELY, LOVE TRULY
AND FORGIVE QUICKLY.

Anonymous

A MAN OF 60 HAS SPENT
20 YEARS IN BED AND
OVER THREE YEARS
IN EATING.

Arnold Bennett

THE MORE YOU PRAISE
AND CELEBRATE YOUR
LIFE, THE MORE
THERE IS IN LIFE TO
CELEBRATE.

Oprah Winfrey

WITH MIRTH AND LAUGHTER LET OLD WRINKLES COME.

William Shakespeare

IF YOU GIVE UP
SMOKING, DRINKING
AND LOVING, YOU DON'T
ACTUALLY LIVE LONGER,
IT JUST SEEMS LONGER.

Clement Freud

AGE DOES NOT DIMINISH
THE EXTREME
DISAPPOINTMENT OF
HAVING A SCOOP OF ICE
CREAM FALL FROM
THE CONE.

Jim Fiebig

DON'T WAIT. MAKE MEMORIES TODAY. CELEBRATE YOUR LIFE!

Anonymous

YOUNG AT HEART

ALTHOUGH IT SOUNDS
ABSURD, IT IS TRUE TO
SAY I FELT YOUNGER AT
60 THAN I FELT AT 20.

Ellen Glasgow

THEY SAY GENES
SKIP GENERATIONS.
MAYBE THAT'S WHY
GRANDPARENTS FIND
THEIR GRANDCHILDREN
SO LIKEABLE.

Joan McIntosh

YOU'RE ONLY AS YOUNG AS THE LAST TIME YOU CHANGED YOUR MIND.

Timothy Leary

THERE IS NO OLD AGE.
THERE IS, AS THERE
ALWAYS WAS, JUST YOU.

Carol Matthau

MY GRANDMOTHER
STARTED WALKING FIVE
MILES A DAY WHEN SHE
WAS 60. SHE'S 97 NOW,
AND WE DON'T KNOW
WHERE THE HELL
SHE IS.

Ellen DeGeneres

I DIDN'T GET OLD ON
PURPOSE, IT JUST
HAPPENED. IF YOU'RE
LUCKY IT COULD
HAPPEN TO YOU.

Andy Rooney

AGEING SEEMS TO BE
THE ONLY AVAILABLE
WAY TO LIVE A
LONG LIFE.

Kitty O'Neill Collins

EVERYONE IS THE AGE OF THEIR HEART.

Guatemalan proverb

AGE IS JUST A
NUMBER. IT'S TOTALLY
IRRELEVANT UNLESS, OF
COURSE, YOU HAPPEN TO
BE A BOTTLE OF WINE.

Joan Collins

WE TURN NOT OLDER WITH YEARS, BUT NEWER EVERY DAY.

Emily Dickinson

AN OLD TIMER IS ONE
WHO REMEMBERS
WHEN WE COUNTED OUR
BLESSINGS INSTEAD OF
OUR CALORIES.

Anonymous

I'M NOT YOUNG ENOUGH TO KNOW EVERYTHING.

Oscar Wilde

MEN DO NOT QUIT
PLAYING BECAUSE THEY
GROW OLD; THEY GROW
OLD BECAUSE THEY
QUIT PLAYING.

Oliver Wendell Holmes Jr

INSIDE EVERY OLDER
PERSON IS A YOUNGER
PERSON — WONDERING
WHAT THE HELL
HAPPENED.

Cora Harvey Armstrong

WE ARE ALWAYS THE SAME AGE INSIDE.

Gertrude Stein

IT TAKES A LONG TIME
TO BECOME YOUNG.

Pablo Picasso

IN OUR DREAMS WE ARE
ALWAYS YOUNG.

Sarah Louise Delany

OLD AGE IS NO PLACE
FOR SISSIES.

Bette Davis

OLDER
AND
WISER?

THEY TOLD ME IF I GOT
OLDER I'D GET WISER. IN
THAT CASE I MUST BE
A GENIUS.

George Burns

IF YOU ARE 60 YEARS
OLD AND HAVE
NO REGRETS, YOU
HAVEN'T LIVED.

Christy Moore

THE ONLY SOURCE OF KNOWLEDGE IS EXPERIENCE.

Albert Einstein

BORN TO BE WILD – LIVE
TO OUTGROW IT.

Doug Horton

THE OLDER I GROW THE
MORE I DISTRUST THE
FAMILIAR DOCTRINE
THAT AGE BRINGS
WISDOM.

H. L. Mencken

THE SECRET TO STAYING
YOUNG IS TO LIVE
HONESTLY, EAT SLOWLY,
AND LIE ABOUT
YOUR AGE.

Lucille Ball

YOU ARE ONLY YOUNG ONCE, BUT YOU CAN BE IMMATURE FOR A LIFETIME.

John P. Grier

I LIVE IN THAT SOLITUDE
WHICH IS PAINFUL IN
YOUTH, BUT DELICIOUS
IN THE YEARS OF
MATURITY.

Albert Einstein

BECOMING A
GRANDMOTHER IS
WONDERFUL. ONE
MOMENT YOU'RE JUST
A MOTHER. THE NEXT
YOU ARE ALL-WISE AND
PREHISTORIC.

Pam Brown

HOW FOOLISH TO THINK
THAT ONE CAN EVER
SLAM THE DOOR IN THE
FACE OF AGE. MUCH
WISER TO BE POLITE AND
GRACIOUS AND ASK HIM
TO LUNCH IN ADVANCE.

Noël Coward

THE MORE SAND HAS
ESCAPED FROM THE
HOURGLASS OF OUR
LIFE, THE CLEARER
WE SHOULD SEE
THROUGH IT.

Jean Paul

WE ARE YOUNG
ONLY ONCE,
AFTER THAT
WE NEED SOME
OTHER EXCUSE.

Anonymous

ONE OF THE GOOD
THINGS ABOUT GETTING
OLDER IS THAT YOU
FIND YOU'RE MORE
INTERESTING THAN
MOST OF THE PEOPLE
YOU MEET.

Lee Marvin

EXPERIENCE IS THE NAME EVERYONE GIVES TO THEIR MISTAKES.

Oscar Wilde

I DON'T WANT TO RETIRE.
I'M NOT THAT GOOD AT
CROSSWORD PUZZLES.

Norman Mailer

THE FIRST 100 YEARS ARE THE HARDEST.

Wilson Mizner

IF I HAD MY LIFE TO
LIVE OVER AGAIN, I
WOULD MAKE THE SAME
MISTAKES, ONLY SOONER.

Tallulah Bankhead

WHEN I WAS A BOY THE DEAD SEA WAS ONLY SICK.

George Burns

LIVE, LOVE AND LAST

PEOPLE ARE ALWAYS
ASKING ABOUT THE
GOOD OLD DAYS. I SAY,
WHY DON'T YOU SAY THE
GOOD NOW DAYS?

Robert M. Young

OLD PEOPLE AREN'T
EXEMPT FROM HAVING
FUN AND DANCING
AND PLAYING.

Liz Smith

HE WHO LAUGHS, LASTS!

Mary Pettibone Poole

LIFE CAN ONLY BE
UNDERSTOOD BACKWARDS;
BUT IT MUST BE LIVED
FORWARDS.

Søren Kierkegaard

YOU ONLY LIVE
ONCE, BUT IF
YOU DO IT RIGHT,
ONCE IS ENOUGH.

Mae West

THERE WAS NO RESPECT
FOR YOUTH WHEN I WAS
YOUNG, AND NOW THAT
I AM OLD, THERE IS NO
RESPECT FOR AGE –
I MISSED IT COMING
AND GOING.

J. B. Priestley

MY ADVICE FOR LIFE:
DANCE AND SING YOUR
SONG WHILE THE PARTY
IS STILL ON.

Rasheed Ogunlaru

MAY YOU LIVE ALL THE DAYS OF YOUR LIFE.

Jonathan Swift

GOD GAVE US THE GIFT
OF LIFE; IT IS UP TO US
TO GIVE OURSELVES THE
GIFT OF LIVING WELL.

Voltaire

TIME DOTH FLIT;
OH SHIT!

Dorothy Parker

LIFE IS JUST ONE GRAND, SWEET SONG, SO START THE MUSIC.

Ronald Reagan

THE KEY TO SUCCESSFUL
AGEING IS TO PAY AS
LITTLE ATTENTION TO IT
AS POSSIBLE.

Judith Regan

THE LONGER I LIVE THE MORE BEAUTIFUL LIFE BECOMES.

Frank Lloyd Wright

THE OLD BEGIN TO
COMPLAIN OF THE
CONDUCT OF THE
YOUNG WHEN THEY
THEMSELVES ARE NO
LONGER ABLE TO SET A
BAD EXAMPLE.

François de La Rochefoucauld

HER BIRTHDAY'S OUR
FETE DAY,
WE'LL MAKE IT OUR
GREAT DAY,
AND GIVE HER OUR
PRESENTS
AND SING HER OUR
SONG.

E. Nesbit

WHEN YOU ARE
DISSATISFIED AND WOULD
LIKE TO GO BACK TO
YOUR YOUTH, THINK OF
ALGEBRA.

Will Rogers

SO MAYST THOU LIVE,
DEAR! MANY YEARS,
IN ALL THE BLISS THAT
LIFE ENDEARS.

Thomas Hood

ILLS,
PILLS
AND
TWINGES

AS YOU GET OLDER
THREE THINGS HAPPEN.
THE FIRST IS YOUR
MEMORY GOES, AND I
CAN'T REMEMBER THE
OTHER TWO...

Norman Wisdom

MY DOCTOR TOLD ME
TO DO SOMETHING
THAT PUTS ME OUT OF
BREATH, SO I'VE TAKEN
UP SMOKING AGAIN.

Jo Brand

EVERYTHING SLOWS
DOWN WITH AGE, EXCEPT
THE TIME IT TAKES
CAKE AND ICE CREAM TO
REACH YOUR HIPS.

John Wagner

GRANT ME CHASTITY AND CONTINENCE, BUT NOT YET.

Augustine of Hippo

I DON'T DO ALCOHOL ANY MORE – I GET THE SAME EFFECT JUST STANDING UP FAST.

Anonymous

I'M AT AN AGE WHEN MY
BACK GOES OUT MORE
THAN I DO.

Phyllis Diller

I'M PUSHING 60. THAT'S ENOUGH EXERCISE FOR ME.

Mark Twain

IF YOU REST, YOU RUST.

Helen Hayes

A HEALTHY OLD FELLOW,
WHO IS NOT A FOOL,
IS THE HAPPIEST
CREATURE LIVING.

Richard Steele

DON'T LET AGEING GET YOU DOWN. IT'S TOO HARD TO GET BACK UP.

John Wagner

THE YEARS BETWEEN
50 AND 70 ARE THE
HARDEST. YOU ARE
ALWAYS BEING ASKED
TO DO MORE, AND YOU
ARE NOT YET DECREPIT
ENOUGH TO TURN
THEM DOWN.

T. S. Eliot

CHIN
UP,
CHEST
OUT

I'M NOT SIXTY, I'M 'SEXTY'!

Dolly Parton

I DON'T PLAN TO GROW
OLD GRACEFULLY; I PLAN
TO HAVE FACELIFTS
UNTIL MY EARS MEET.

Rita Rudner

MIDDLE AGE IS WHEN
A NARROW WAIST AND A
BROAD MIND BEGIN TO
CHANGE PLACES.

Anonymous

I HAVE A FURNITURE
PROBLEM. MY CHEST
HAS FALLEN INTO MY
DRAWERS.

Billy Casper

I'VE ONLY GOT ONE
WRINKLE AND I'M
SITTING ON IT.

Jeanne Calment

LET US RESPECT GREY HAIRS, ESPECIALLY OUR OWN.

J. P. Sears

LOOKING 50 IS GREAT — IF YOU'RE 60.

Joan Rivers

SOME PEOPLE, NO
MATTER HOW OLD THEY
GET, NEVER LOSE THEIR
BEAUTY – THEY MERELY
MOVE IT FROM THEIR
FACES INTO THEIR
HEARTS.

Martin Buxbaum

YOU CAN ONLY PERCEIVE REAL BEAUTY IN A PERSON AS THEY GET OLDER.

Anouk Aimée

THERE IS MORE
FELICITY ON THE FAR
SIDE OF BALDNESS
THAN YOUNG MEN CAN
POSSIBLY IMAGINE.

Logan Pearsall Smith

EXPERIENCE IS A COMB
THAT LIFE GIVES YOU
AFTER YOU LOSE
YOUR HAIR.

Judith Stern

YEARS MAY WRINKLE
THE SKIN, BUT TO
GIVE UP ENTHUSIASM
WRINKLES THE SOUL.

Samuel Ullman

TO WIN BACK MY YOUTH...
THERE IS NOTHING I
WOULDN'T DO — EXCEPT
TAKE EXERCISE, GET UP
EARLY, OR BE A USEFUL
MEMBER OF THE
COMMUNITY.

Oscar Wilde

INFLATION IS WHEN YOU
PAY 15 DOLLARS FOR THE
10-DOLLAR HAIRCUT YOU
USED TO GET FOR
FIVE DOLLARS WHEN
YOU HAD HAIR.

Sam Ewing

TIME MAY BE A GREAT
HEALER, BUT IT'S A
LOUSY BEAUTICIAN.

Anonymous

AN ARCHAEOLOGIST IS
THE BEST HUSBAND
ANY WOMAN CAN HAVE:
THE OLDER SHE GETS,
THE MORE INTERESTED
HE IS IN HER.

Agatha Christie

DON'T RETOUCH MY
WRINKLES IN THE
PHOTOGRAPH... I
WOULD NOT WANT IT
TO BE THOUGHT THAT
I HAD LIVED FOR ALL
THESE YEARS WITHOUT
SOMETHING TO SHOW
FOR IT.

Queen Elizabeth, The Queen Mother

IT IS NOT HOW OLD YOU ARE, BUT HOW YOU ARE OLD.

Marie Dressler

@EsmeTheBird

If you're interested in finding out more about our books, find us on Facebook at **Summersdale Publishers** and follow us on Twitter at **@Summersdale**.

www.summersdale.com